SIMPLY SCIENCE

Water

by Alice K. Flanagan

Content Adviser: Terrence E. Young Jr., M.Ed., M.L.S.,
Jefferson Parish (La.) Public Schools

Reading Adviser: Dr. Linda D. Labbo,
Department of Reading Education, College of Education,
The University of Georgia

 COMPASS POINT BOOKS

Minneapolis, Minnesota

Compass Point Books
3109 West 50th Street, #115
Minneapolis, MN 55410

Visit Compass Point Books on the Internet at *www.compasspointbooks.com* or e-mail your
request to *custserv@compasspointbooks.com*

Editors: E. Russell Primm, Emily J. Dolbear, and Melissa Stewart
Photo Researcher: Svetlana Zhurkina
Photo Selector: Dawn Friedman
Design: Bradfordesign, Inc.

Library of Congress Cataloging-in-Publication Data

Flanagan, Alice K.
    Water / by Alice K. Flanagan.
        p. cm. — (Simply science)
    Includes bibliographical references (p.   ) and index.
    Summary: Describes the forms water takes, how it has shaped Earth, and its importance to life.
    ISBN 0-7565-0038-9 (hardcover : lib. bdg.)
      1. Water—Juvenile literature. [1. Water.] I. Title. II. Simply science (Minneapolis, Minn.)
    GB662.3 .F59 2000
    551.46—dc21
                                                                   00-008577

Table of Contents

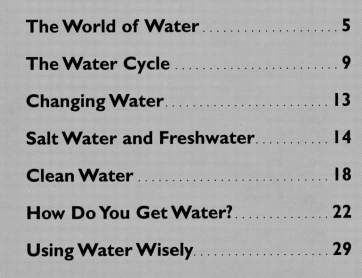

The World of Water

Walk in the rain. Drink from a tap. Swim in a lake. Cry a tear. Water is so important in our lives. We cannot live without water.

Water is found inside every living thing. It is in our bodies and in the air we breathe. It is in the ground and in the seas. More than 70 percent of Earth is covered with the water of oceans, rivers,

Rain is water.

Tears are water.

and lakes. And more than half of the human body is made up of water. Some plants and animals spend their entire lives in water. Water puts out fires, produces electricity, and carries boats.

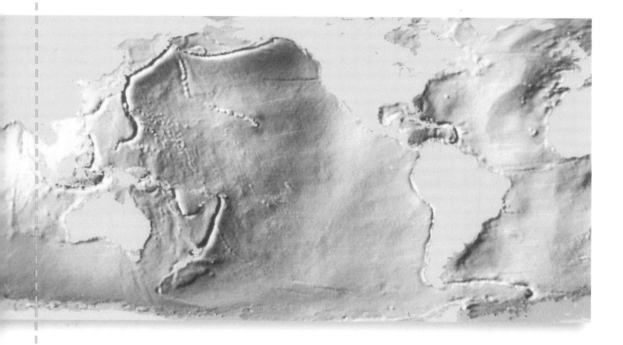

◀ A map of the world's oceans

Playing along the ocean's shore ▶
is fun!

The Water Cycle

The water you see today is the same water that was on Earth millions of years ago. Water can be used over and over again. This is called the water cycle.

The water cycle begins when the sun dries up puddles and heats the water in lakes,

Elephants need water from lakes to drink and keep cool.

Riverboats carry people down the Mississippi River.

rivers, and oceans. As the water heats up, it rises into the air as a **gas** called **water vapor**.

When water vapor rises, it cools and turns into tiny water droplets. The droplets form clouds that move across the sky. When the droplets get heavy, they fall back to Earth as rain. If the air is cold, the rain may turn into sleet or hail or snow.

Some of the water from rain, snow, hail, and sleet soaks into the **soil**. The rest of the water

Clouds are formed by water droplets.

moves across the land and flows into rivers, lakes, and oceans.

Then the water cycle starts again. The sun heats up the water and it rises into the air as water vapor. The water cycle goes on forever.

People need to drink water to replace the water lost by sweating.

Humans are part of the water cycle. Our bodies take in water from food and drink. We lose water when we sweat. Sweat may fall to the ground and soak into the soil, or it may rise into the air as water vapor.

Ice is frozen water.

Water as a liquid

Changing Water

Water is always changing. It can be a **liquid**, a **solid**, or a gas. The water that you drink or bathe in is a liquid. You can pour it or splash in it.

If you put a pot of water in the freezer, it will change into ice. Ice is a solid. If you heat the pot on the stove, the ice will change back to liquid water. If you keep heating the pot, you will see the liquid water turn into a gas. Watch the water vapor, or steam, as it rises.

Boiling water turns to steam. ▶

Salt Water and Freshwater

Nearly all the water on Earth is salt water, or ocean water. Can you name all the oceans in the world? Which ocean is the largest?

Ocean water is too salty to drink. When ocean water warms up and changes into water vapor, the salt is left behind. The salt does not rise into the air. So when the water falls back to Earth as rain, it is freshwater.

We need clean freshwater to live and grow. But Earth has only a small amount of freshwater. Most of the freshwater is frozen at the North and

The Pacific Ocean is the world's largest ocean.

Mountains covered in snow and ice in Antarctica

South Poles. We cannot use this water.

The rest of the freshwater is found in rivers and lakes or underground. **Groundwater** is cleaner than the water in most lakes and rivers. People dig holes, or wells, in the ground to reach the groundwater. Many people use groundwater every day to drink, wash, and cook.

An iceberg in Antarctica

A freshwater lake in the mountains

Clean Water

The droplets of water that make up clouds are clean water. When the drops falls to Earth as rain, they pick up dust and dangerous materials in the air.

Even the water in this stream may contain dangerous materials.

This winding river picks up pollutants as it flows toward the ocean.

When the rain reaches land, it picks up other things that are not safe. Waste materials from factories and farms get into the water as it flows into rivers and lakes. This makes the water dirty, or **polluted**. Plants that take in polluted water may die. Animals need clean water too. So do we.

Polluted water kills fish.

A factory pipe dumps chemicals into the water.

How Do You Get Water?

Do you know where your water comes from? Some people get their water from wells near their house. Other people get their water from a nearby lake.

You probably get your water from a very large well or lake that is far away. That well or lake contains

Irrigation sprinklers water a field.

We can get fresh water just by turning on a faucet.

enough water to supply all the people in your town. Before the water gets to your house, it has to be cleaned, or treated, at a treatment plant.

The clean water is pumped into tanks or water towers. It is stored there until people need it. When you turn on a faucet, the water goes through under- ground pipes to your house.

◀ *A town's water is sometimes stored in big water towers.*

Wells are dug to bring water ▶ *out of the ground.*

Then you can have a drink of good clean water.

Used water runs through pipes from your house to a place where it is cleaned. Then it is probably pumped back into a river or lake. When it is properly cleaned, water may be used again and again.

Water treatment tanks clean water.

A man takes a water sample for testing.

Using Water Wisely

Plants and other animals cannot clean polluted water. They depend on people to keep freshwater clean. We should never dump waste into rivers, lakes, or ponds. We should also protect our oceans and the plants and animals that live in them. The world has only a certain amount of water. Without it, all living things would die. We must use water wisely.

Our oceans need our protection.

Animals need clean water. ▶

Glossary

gas—a substance like air that spreads to fill any space. You can't see most gases.

groundwater—water below the ground that supplies wells and springs

liquid—a wet substance that you can pour. A liquid takes on the shape of the container it is in.

polluted—dirty or dangerous air or water

soil—a mixture of broken-up rock and bits of dead plants and animals

solid—a material that has its own shape and is usually hard

water vapor—water that has turned into a gas. It is also called steam.

Did You Know?

- Some parts of the ocean are almost 7 miles (11 kilometers) deep.

- The basilisk lizard, the western grebe, the fisher spider, the water strider, and the rove beetle can all walk on water.

- More than 25,000 kinds of fish live in the world. The largest fish— the whale shark— is longer than two school buses. The smallest fish—the goby— is about the size of the eraser on a pencil.

Want to Know More?

At the Library

Challoner, Jack. *Wet and Dry*. Austin, Tex.: Raintree Steck-Vaughn, 1997.

Wick, Walter. *A Drop of Water: A Book of Science and Wonder*. New York: Scholastic, 1997.

Williams, John. *Water Projects*. Austin, Tex.: Raintree Steck-Vaughn, 1998.

On the Web

The Water Cycle

http://www.epa.state.il.us/kids/fun-stuff/water-cycle

To make your own water cycle wheel

Water in the City

http://www.fi.edu/city/water/

For information about water basics, water supplies, and water activities

Through the Mail

Soil and Water Conservation Society

7515 NE Ankeny Road

Ankeny, IA 50021

For information about soil and water management and the environment

On the Road

SeaWorld

7007 SeaWorld Drive

Orlando, FL 32821

800/327-2424

To learn about the ocean and a variety of ocean animals. SeaWorlds are also located in Ohio, California, and Texas.

Index

About the Author

Alice K. Flanagan writes books for children and teachers. Ever since she was a young girl, she has enjoyed writing. She has written more than seventy books on a wide variety of topics. Some of her books include biographies of U.S. presidents and their wives, biographies of people working in our neighborhoods, phonics books for beginning readers, and informational books about birds and Native Americans. Alice K. Flanagan lives in Chicago, Illinois.